I am
Harriet Tubman

adapted by Marilyn Easton

PENGUIN YOUNG READERS LICENSES
An Imprint of Penguin Random House LLC, New York

Published in 2021 by Penguin Young Readers Licenses, an imprint of Penguin Random House LLC, New York. Manufactured in China.

Visit us online at www.penguinrandomhouse.com.

ISBN 9780593225813   10 9 8 7 6 5 4 3 2 1

One afternoon at the museum, Xavier, his sister Yadina, and their friend Brad were trying to decide who the best superhero of all time was.

"One thing is for sure, whoever it is needs to have courage. That means they're not scared of anything," said Xavier.

Then they heard a loud crash and went to investigate.

"Mom and Dad are working on a new exhibit," Xavier said.
"I wonder what's down there!"

"That hall is too scary," Yadina said.

"Too bad we aren't superheroes. Then we'd have enough courage," said Xavier.

At that, a blue portal opened right under their feet. The friends disappeared!

The portal led to the Secret Museum.

"Maybe we're meeting a superhero!" cheered Xavier.

An image of Harriet Tubman appeared. The Secret Museum was sending them to Maryland in 1833. They placed their hands on Berby and traveled back in time!

"So this is Maryland in 1833?" Xavier wondered.

"It would be really nice to have a superhero right about now," said Yadina, feeling nervous.

"Yeah, someone who isn't scared of anything," Xavier agreed.

Suddenly, Harriet appeared!

"Hope I didn't scare you," Harriet whispered. "We need to be quiet. I'm going to see my family."

"At night?" asked Xavier.

"By yourself?" asked Brad.

"Yes. You can come if you like, but we have to hurry," replied Harriet.

Harriet led them through the woods. It was very dark!

"How do you know where to go?" Brad asked.

"I use the sky as a map," Harriet explained. "That big bright star is called the North Star because it always leads north. That's where my family is."

Soon they arrived at a clearing where Harriet's family was waiting for her. It had been a long time since Harriet had seen them.

Harriet introduced her new friends to her family.

"Nice to meet you!" Yadina said. "But I have a question. You're a family, so . . . aren't you together all the time?"

"Here, if you have skin that looks like ours, you aren't always free to do what you like," Harriet explained. "People can enslave you and tell you what to do. They can keep you away from your family. We get in a lot of trouble if we don't follow the rules."

Xavier, Yadina, and Brad were sad. They couldn't imagine being kept away from their families.

"We shouldn't have to sneak out at night to be together. We should be free," said Harriet's mom, Rit.

"So, that's why you were being so quiet on the way here," Xavier realized.

Harriet nodded.

"It's a good thing you have so much courage," Rit said to Harriet. "Real courage is bravely moving forward even when you're scared."

Suddenly, a meteor shower brightened up the sky.
Harriet and her family watched together, hand in hand.

"I wonder if Harriet and her family will ever get to do what they want, and be together all the time," said Brad.

"And live free, like people do today," Xavier said.

Suddenly, Berby appeared. With a flash, the friends traveled in time again.

They arrived in Maryland in 1857. Harriet was there!

"Why are you dressed like that?" Yadina asked her.

"It's a disguise, so people won't recognize me. I finally escaped from slavery. I'm free now," Harriet explained.

"If you're free, why did you come back?" Xavier asked.

"There are so many people who aren't free. I come back to help them," said Harriet.

"That sounds dangerous!" Brad said.

"It is, but it's the right thing to do. I helped my brothers escape, and tonight I'm going to save my parents," Harriet said.

"Talk about a superhero!" Yadina said.

"Aren't you scared?" Xavier asked.

"Of course. Everyone gets scared sometimes," Harriet explained. "Fear reminds us to look out for danger."

In the dark of night, Harriet led her parents across bumpy trails and through the woods.

"To be safe, we can only travel at night," said Harriet. "My friend lives there. We'll stop and rest for the day at his house."

Once day turned to night, they continued their difficult journey through rivers and over plains. More days and nights passed, and they still continued on.

"Where to next?" asked Yadina.

"Home," replied Harriet.

When the sun rose the next day, Harriet took her family to freedom.

"We're safe now," said Harriet as she and her parents reunited with the rest of their family. "We're free."

"I think I know why the Secret Museum sent us here," said Xavier.

"Me too! Harriet Tubman is the ultimate superhero," said Yadina. "She had more courage than anyone ever."

Just then, Berby appeared. It was time for the friends to go home, too.

Back at the museum, they walked through the scary hall together and went to explore the exhibit.

It was dedicated to the heroes of the Underground Railroad.

Xavier read from a plaque: "The Underground Railroad was a secret group of brave individuals who helped people escape from slavery to freedom. One of their leaders was . . ."

"Harriet Tubman!" cheered Xavier, Yadina, and Brad.
With or without a cape, Harriet would always be a real-life superhero.